New Hampshire's
# WHITE MOUNTAINS
and
# LAKES REGION

# New Hampshire's
# WHITE MOUNTAINS
## and
# LAKES REGION

Photographs by
## Robert J. Kozlow

Huntington Graphics
Burlington, Vermont

Published by Huntington Graphics
Copyright © 2015 Huntington Graphics
Copyright © 2015 Photographs Robert J. Kozlow

Cover Design by Andrea Gray
Book Layout & Design by John Hadden

Cover Photo: Aerial view of Squam Lake with Mount Washington in the distance.
Back Cover: Durand Lake in Randolph.

Printed in China

Huntington Graphics
PO Box 373, Burlington, VT 05402
www.huntingtongraphics.com

ISBN 978-1-886064-48-5

# Contents

# Acknowledgements

Many people were instrumental in the creation of this book. Jared Gange, my publisher, and his designer, John Hadden, spent many hours pouring over the digital image files to provide a striking representation of the lakes and mountains of New Hampshire. Andrea Gray created a cover concept to best compliment the theme of lakes and mountains. Chris Whiton reviewed all of the chosen images and adjusted them for proper printing resolution.

I would like to take the time to recognize the employees of the New Hampshire State Park System as well as the many people who operate our tourist attractions. In particular, I'd like to thank Mike Pelchat, Bill and Jayne O'Connor, Amy Bassett, Howie Wemyss, and Dr. Peter Crane who have assisted me in getting to certain photographic locations on short notice.

Special thanks go to all my friends who have helped me with various photo shoots and who appear as models throughout this book. Most notably, I'd like to thank Andrew and Patrick Keefer, Chris Whiton, Mark Hollenbach, Joel Quiggin, Jack Varin, Chris O'Leary, Eben Alexander, Jared Alden, Cody Cook, Dr. Troy Schrupp, Jack and Tessa Schrupp, Andrew Rebeiro, Zak Fitts, Shaun Moe, and Nate Suggs.

I would also like to thank John Anderson, Staci Schoenrock, and Dave Emerson of Emerson Aviation for assistance in obtaining the aerial photos, and Tod Campbell for helping me obtain loon photos.

I am very fortunate to have professional colleagues who have supported me through all of my photography projects. In particular, I would like to thank the Dental Resource Center at LRGHealthcare and my Meredith dental office staff. Thank you, Kelly Beddia, for being a good listener and a faithful friend.

Thank you, Chris Whiton, for your technical photographic expertise and your friendship in allowing me to "tag along" on many hiking bushwacks that have given me the opportunity to photograph some very unique and breathtaking waterfalls and scenic vistas known only to a small group of explorers.

Finally, I would like to dedicate this book to my parents, the late Donna and Joseph Kozlow, whose unconditional love, patience, and encouragement made all of this possible. It has truly been a labor of love on many wonderful journeys through God's Country.

Robert J. Kozlow
Gilford, New Hampshire

Facing page: *Loon Island casts its reflection in the calm morning water of Newfound Lake.*

# Preface

As a transplant from southeastern Michigan, I consider my years in New Hampshire to be a blessing and a privilege. Very few photographers have the good fortune to live, work and play in an area that presents unlimited photographic opportunities. This book is a labor of love that started over twenty years ago and has only grown stronger with time.

I distinctly remember my first trip to the Flume in Franconia Notch State Park. I immediately became obsessed with the White Mountains. Every weekend was spent visiting different nooks and crannies in the northern part of the state. When I relocated to practice dentistry in the Lakes Region, I was quickly introduced to the natural jewels in that area, my favorite being Squam Lake. I was fortunate to have a number of friends who invited me on their boats to explore some of the more intimate and unique coves on Squam.

My parents always thought that my passion for New Hampshire would be short-lived, but it only grew stronger with each passing year. The Lakes Region, White Mountains and the Great North Woods are without question our most popular tourist destinations, and I truly believe that one must experience these beautiful regions in all four seasons. Many of the photos in this book are the result of repeated trips to the same location to capture a different mood or feeling.

This poem by Henry David Thoreau best describes my feelings for New Hampshire.

*I long for wilderness*
*woods where the wood thrush*
*forever sings*
*where the hours are early*
*morning ones*
*and the dew is on the grass*
*and the day is forever*
*unproven*
*a New Hampshire everlasting*
*and unfallen.*

Robert J. Kozlow
May 2015

Facing page: *From Zeacliff, looking across the Pemigewasset Wilderness to Mount Carrigain.*

# Introduction

New Hampshire is blessed with many options for recreation, vacationing and sightseeing. From its undeveloped Great North Woods, to the peaks and rivers of the White Mountains, to the lakes large and small in the Lakes Region, to its southern seacoast beaches, there is something here for everyone to enjoy. This book covers the immensely popular White Mountains and the summer paradise of the Lakes Region. While each region has its own distinct landscape—the one characterized by lakes and low, scattered mountains, the other a rugged, forested mountain mass with deep valleys carved by glaciers—we group them together because the mountainous northern rim of the Lakes Region forms the southern edge of the White Mountains.

*Squam Lake's many islands are captured in this aerial view on an exceptionally clear summer's day.*

*Aerial view of Franconia Ridge with Lonesome Lake in the foreground and Mount Washington and the Presidentials in the distance.*

Facing page: *Weirs Beach from the air, looking out over Lake Winnipesaukee,*
*with Governor's Island partially shown on the right side of the image.*

*Tuckerman Ravine, famous for spring skiing, still retains some snow in June.*

Facing page: *Looking north along Franconia Ridge. From top to bottom: Mount Lafayette, Mount Lincoln, and Little Haystack. The hike along this high, open ridge is one of the finest in the eastern United States.*

*Aerial view of the Northern Presidential Range with Mount Washington in the center and Mount Adams and Mount Madison in the distance. The cliffs of Tuckerman and Huntington Ravines are visible to the right of Mount Washington's summit.*

*Aerial view of Sunapee Harbor. Lake Sunapee, located 40 miles southwest of Lake Winnipesaukee, offers superb swimming and boating in crystal clear waters.*

*In this aerial view, taken above Cannon Mountain, Lonesome Lake nestles in the foreground and ski runs spill down into Franconia Notch. Across I-93, the Franconia Range is on full display, from Mount Lafayette to distant Mount Flume. Bondcliff and the Pemigewasset Wilderness lie beyond.*

*Facing page: Late summer view of Paugus Bay and Lake Winnipesaukee. Weirs Beach is seen in the center of the image.*

# In and Around the Lakes Region

Located about 40 miles north of Concord, New Hampshire's Lakes Region boasts over 250 lakes and ponds and is a major boating, fishing, paddling and swimming destination. Summer homes and "camps" of all sizes and vintages line the shorelines and perch on islands. Two lakes receive most of the attention, Squam Lake and Lake Winnipesaukee. Smaller Squam Lake offers a less developed, more laid-back scene, where many camps have been in the same family for generations. Much larger Lake Winnipesaukee provides more options for the boater, and the towns of Meredith, Center Harbor, Alton Bay and Wolfeboro offer the full gamut of services to summer vacationers: shops, restaurants, hotels, marinas and lake cruises. In June, the annual Laconia Motorcycle Week draws over 100,000 motorcyclists to Weirs Beach and the surrounding region.

*A light breeze on Squam Lake makes for a good sailing day.*

*An unusually homey fishing shanty on Meredith Bay, Lake Winnipesaukee.*

Facing page: *On a less obviously wintery note, a Christmas tree on a dock in Gilford lets us know what the season is.*

*Lake Winnipesaukee's many islands are home to hundreds of summer camps.*

*Weirs Channel is a key link between Paugus Bay and Lake Winnipesaukee.*

*Early morning calm on Lake Winnipesaukee before summer activities get underway.*

*Loons, like most water birds, need to shake water from their feathers from time to time.*

*Once owned by a former governor of New Hampshire, Highland View Farm in East Andover boasts this magnificent barn.*

Facing page: *High above Lake Winnipesaukee, Castle in the Clouds, a popular summer destination, basks in the sun. The attractions include waterfalls, gardens and miles of hiking trails.*

*Nowadays, the sap for making maple syrup is usually collected using plastic tubing. The old method using sap buckets is shown on the tree in the foreground.*

*Facing page: Hues of orange and purple shape the mood in this sunrise view of Indian Island, Meredith Bay, with its iconic statue of Chief Chocorua.*

*This boathouse on Little Squam Lake in Holderness was featured in the movie, "On Golden Pond".*

*A barn in Hebron, in the bright sun of late winter, with Newfound Lake visible in the background. Hebron is an old-fashioned village complete with post office, meeting house and general store.*

*Since 1940, the M/V Mount Washington has provided summer vacationers a great way to relax and see Lake Winnipesaukee.*

*Preceeding page left: A classic summer camp on the shores of Little Lake Sunapee basks in the late day summer sun.*

*Preceeding page right: The stillness of this scene hints at the timelessness of the well-preserved village of Center Sandwich.*

*Each June, the town of Meredith hosts the Wooden Boat Regatta, showcasing antique boats from all over New England.*

*Winter ice forms early in narrow Alton Bay, at the southeastern edge of Lake Winnipesaukee.*

*The quintessential New England town of Meredith is nicely situated at the northwest corner of Lake Winnipesaukee. With its many stores, restaurants, and hotels, Meredith is one of the Lake Region's main attractions.*

*The old mill site on the Squam River in Ashland near Plymouth.*

*Full moon over Red Hill on Squaw Cove, Squam Lake, on a particularly calm evening.*

# In and Around the White Mountains

The White Mountains are the premier destination in New England for mountain scenery. With 48 mountains exceeding 4,000 feet, it is a vast resource for hiking, river paddling, cycling, climbing, skiing and snowmobiling. For those inclined to less strenuous pursuits, views of waterfalls, covered bridges, mountains and most popular of all, its world-famous fall foliage, are accessible to all. Most of the region is included in the White Mountain National Forest, and as such is really one enormous forest, some of it designated as wilderness. The highest peak, Mount Washington, is accessible by car, by cog railway and by hiking trails. The few highways that pass through these mountains offer spectacular views of glacial valleys, high cliffs and rushing rivers. The gateway towns of Littleton, Lincoln, Gorham and especially North Conway, provide accommodations, restaurants and shopping to meet every taste and budget.

*The view south along spectacular Franconia Ridge, from its highest point, 5,280-foot Mount Lafayette. Two ski runs on Loon Mountain are visible in the distance, left of the rocky summit of Mount Lincoln.*

*From Mount Lincoln, looking out across the Pemigewasset Wilderness to Mount Carrigain.*

*Facing page: The coal-fired cog railway on Mount Washington's west side is the second steepest cog railway in the world. Shown here is Jacob's Ladder, the steepest grade, at 37%.*

*Holiday lights brighten up the covered bridge in the village of Stark. Located in New Hampshire's remote North Country, Stark housed German prisoners during World War II.*

*As seen from Cannon Mountain's frosty summit, the late afternoon light creates the alpenglow effect on Mount Lafayette and Mount Lincoln. Below the ridge, Walker Ravine is already in evening shadow.*

*Unknown Pond is a North Country gem. The Horn, a 3,904-foot mountain peak in the Pilot Range, rises in the background.*

*An easy trail leads to the shore of Cherry Pond. In the distance, the Presidential Range sprawls across the horizon.*

*The icy slopes of Mount Washington gleam in the early morning sunlight. The ski runs on Wildcat Mountain are idle this early in the day.*

*The Flume Covered Bridge in Franconia Notch was built in 1886. It spans the Pemigewasset River, and a Christmas wreath adorns the bridge every winter.*

*From Mount Washington's summit cone, looking south over Lakes of the Clouds and the Appalachian Mountain Club's hut.*
*A "sea of clouds" has formed to the west of Mount Monroe and the Southern Presidential Range.*

*A moderate hike out of Franconia Notch leads to peaceful Lonesome Lake reflecting the Franconia Ridge in a foliage season featuring both snow and color.*

*Bretton Woods' historic Mount Washington Hotel dates from 1902. Visitors can relax and enjoy the views or partake of any number of outdoor activities, summer and winter, from golf to skiing.*

*Close-up view of ice feathers and rime on the old Summit Stage House on the top of Mount Washington—one of the stormiest places on the planet—on a calm and sunny day.*

*A full-grown bull moose can be up to seven feet at the shoulder and weigh 1000 to 1200 pounds.*

Facing page: *Saco Lake reflecting Mount
Webster and Mount Willard in Crawford Notch.*

*Well north of the White Mountain National Forest, lovely Dixville Notch and historic Balsams Resort, show early signs of fall.*

Facing page: *Nestled high in Great Gulf, tiny Spaulding Lake is one of the highest and most remote bodies of water in the White Mountains.*

*Jefferson Meadows in full winter dress. The Northern Presidential Range is in the background.*

*There is not much warmth in this mid-winter view of Great Gulf and the Northern "Presies", taken a short distance below the summit of Mount Washington. The Northern Presidentials are comprised of Mount Clay, Mount Jefferson, Mount Adams and most distant, Mount Madison.*

*The classic east side view of Mount Washington from Wildcat Mountain with Tuckerman Ravine on the left and Huntington Ravine on the right.*

*Sunset on a cold and wintry day from the summit of Mount Washington.*

# Summer Activities

Whether it be taking a cruise on Lake Winnipesaukee, stepping back in time in the historic village of Center Sandwich, shopping in Meredith, swimming in the remarkably clear water of Newfound Lake, kayaking on Squam Lake or enjoying the view from the top of Mount Major, there is something here for almost every taste in the Lakes Region.

Moving north, Squam Lake's Mt. Morgan and Mt. Percival are soon replaced by the higher peaks of Waterville Valley, followed by the Pemigewasset Wilderness and finally the Presidential Range and Mount Washington. Along the way, hikers can hike the Appalachian Trail, staying at high-mountain, full service huts. The Saco, Pemigewasset and Swift Rivers offer wonderful swimming and paddling, and cyclists have everything from bike paths to steep mountain highways at their disposal.

*Reached by a relatively short hike, the views of Lake Winnipesaukee from Mount Major's summit make this a worthy goal for any hiker.*

*Two paddlers set out across Chocorua Lake, heading in the direction of Mount Chocorua.*

*Smaller than its neighbor, Lake Winnipesaukee, Lake Waukewan offers a more tranquil, laid back summer scene.*

*Swimmers prepare for the Bear Island ritual: when the mail boat, Sophie S., departs, they jump off the pilings into the water!*

*Facing page: These motorcyclists check out Weirs Beach in the early morning calm. Weirs Beach hosts Laconia Motorcycle Week which attracts many thousands of cyclists every year.*

*A beautiful example of the old Chris Craft style wooden boat makes its dignified approach to Wolfeboro. Wolfeboro, together with Meredith, on the other side of the lake, are the two main hubs of activity on Lake Winnipesaukee.*

*Standup paddling at sunrise on Squam Lake.*

*A favorite jumping rock in Rattlesnake Cove, Squam Lake.*

*A leisurely drift down the Saco River is a favorite pastime for summer visitors to North Conway.*

*Enjoying the calm waters of early morning on Squam Lake. West Rattlesnake Mountain is in the background.*

Facing page: *A wonderful way to launch into Lake Winnipesaukee.*

*The classic view of Franconia Notch showing Echo Lake and Cannon Mountain. The hikers are on Artist's Bluff, reached by a short climb from the road.*

*Facing page: A mellow paddle on Echo Lake, North Conway. Whitehorse Ledge, in the background, offers a much more strenuous and vertical option for the rock climber.*

*High on Mount Washington, a hiker works his way across the top of Tuckerman Ravine. The cairns are essential to route finding in foggy conditions.*

Facing page: *Deep in the Pemigewasset Wilderness, a hiker stands on one of the most remote summits in the White Mountains, Bondcliff.*

*Just off the Appalachian Trail, two young hikers and their dad contemplate Mount Flume from the summit of Mount Liberty.*

*Facing page: The snow in Tuckerman Ravine is almost gone now, but in the early spring the snow reaches depths of twenty feet or more.*

*The Rattlesnake cliffs in Rumney have become an international sport climbing destination in recent years.*

*Two hikers approach Lakes of the Clouds Hut. Located in the saddle between Mount Washington and Mount Monroe, "Lakes" is the highest hut in the White Mountains at 5,050 feet.*

# Flowers

In the spring and summer, New Hampshire explodes with color, in over 250 ways! From the state flower, the lilac, to fields of lupines, to cotton sedge in high mountain bogs, New Hampshire's variety of wildflowers is amazing. Few states have the range of habitat from temperate seacoast to sub-arctic mountaintops, with woodlands, meadows, and wetlands—both forested and open—in between. Among the favorites are Chicory, Lapland Rosebay, Bluets, Purple-fringed Orchids, Coneflower, Painted Trillium, Yellow Lady's Slipper, Wild Calla Lily, Wintergreen and Alpine Azalea.

*Lilacs are the official state flower of New Hampshire. Many shrubs come into bloom during late May such as these on Sugar Hill. Mount Layfayette boasts a late spring blanket of snow.*

*Lupines are widespread in the White Mountains in early June. This field is in Randolph, on the west side of Mount Washington.*

Facing page: *One of the first flowers to appear in the spring,*
*Painted Trillium, nestles among the roots of a yellow birch.*

*Lichen-covered rock and alpine azalea in mid-June at high elevation in the White Mountains.*

*Near the summit of Mount Washington, alpine flowers have their day in the warm sun of early June. Mount Adams and Mount Madison peek through the clouds.*

*Day lilies bask in the lowland summer warmth of Randolph, while the 5,000-foot summits of Mount Madison and Mount Adams keep their cool.*

*Lupines wait for the sun to burn off the morning mist on Sugar Hill.*

*Thousand-foot high Cannon Cliff defines the western edge of Franconia Notch. A field of daisies on the valley floor softens the towering wall of granite.*

*The Prescott Farm Audubon Center in Laconia shows a spring display of daffodils.*

*Pink Lady Slippers and Starflowers are found on many valley trails in late spring and early summer.*

*A colorful meadow of buttercups surrounds Iris Farm in Sugar Hill.*

# Fall

Starting around the middle of September, and lasting about a month, the forests of New Hampshire seem to catch fire. Visitors come from all over the world to witness the annual transformation of green hillsides to great swaths of magenta, red, orange and yellow. Starting in the north and at higher elevations, this wave of color gradually migrates south and to the lower elevations. Poplars, elms and birches start off, followed by maples with their spectacular reds and yellows. The show concludes with oaks and beeches. For many this is the time to visit. Begin in the north and follow the show south.

*Fall foliage at its best on Zealand Pond.*

*Cherry Pond on a remarkably calm day during peak foliage. Cherry Mountain is in the foreground, Mount Washington and the Presidential Range are in the distance.*

*While millions have admired the fall foliage in Franconia Notch, very few have seen it from this perspective! Cannon Mountain Ski Area is almost directly below, while Franconia Ridge stretches out on the left side of the image.*

*Fall foliage seen from Bald Ledge above peaceful Lake Winona in New Hampton.*

*A classic New England scene with the fall harvest spread out beneath an old maple tree.*

*Saco Lake in Crawford Notch, with Mount Webster in the distance.*

*The cliffs of Mount Webster tower over Route 302 in Crawford Notch. Saco Lake is visible at the left edge, and Mount Washington is the high point in the center of the image.*

*From Clarksville in the North Country, looking west to Vermont's Mount Monadnock.*

*Located near Colebrook, Beaver Brook Falls is impressive in this autumn scene.*

*There is a fall mood in the valley, but high on Mount Washington early winter is already there. This is the view from the Eisenhower Wayside Park, a little south of Bretton Woods.*

*A fly fisherman tries his luck in Saco Lake, Crawford Notch, on a fine autumn afternoon.*

*An autumn landscape in the North Country, with First Connecticut Lake and Mount Magalloway.*

*Little Hellgate Falls is near Mount Magalloway, well north of the White Mountains. During the annual spring log drives, years ago, Hellgate Falls lived up to its name as a notorious bottleneck.*

*The little village of Tamworth in its fall glory.*

Facing page: *Sentinel Pine Covered Bridge in Franconia Notch. The bridge rests on the trunk of a huge pine tree, felled by the Great Hurricane of 1938.*

*Fall foliage on West Rattlesnake overlooking Squam Lake, a spot accessible by a short one-mile hike.*

*Beaver Pond in Kinsman Notch on an extremely calm late September morning.*

# Waterfalls

While not among the country's highest or most powerful, New Hampshire's many waterfalls and cascades are noteworthy for their variety. Over thousands of years, the abundant rainfall and spring snowmelt of the White Mountains combined with steep mountain slopes has created a range of delights. From quirky pools carved in granite bedrock to 200-foot high cascades to plunging waterfalls, the area seems to have it all. On the mellower slopes in the Lakes Region, small waterfalls and cascades wind over and around mossy boulders leaving calm pools and deep swimming holes in their wake.

*Rainbow Falls can be reached by a three-quarter mile hike into the Walter/Newton Natural Area in Plymouth.*

*This small flume is a miniature version of the famous Flume Gorge in Franconia Notch State Park.*

*Beaver Brook Cascades are found along a one-mile stretch of the Beaver Brook Trail, a challenging portion of the Appalachian Trail that climbs to the summit of Mount Moosilauke.*

*After hiking part way up Falling Waters Trail in Franconia Notch, spectacular Cloudland Falls is a great spot to take a break, especially on a warm day.*

*Shocked by the cold water of Arethusa Falls, a swimmer contemplates his next move.*

*On the King Ravine Trail, a young hiker has picked a uniquely beautiful spot to study the guide book before proceeding.*

*A short side trail from the Ammonoosuc Ravine Trail leads to this spectacular cascade. The Ammonoosuc Ravine Trail is the main ascent route of Mount Washington from the west.*

*A well-engineered stone walkway leads visitors to the base of 70-foot Glen Ellis Falls in Pinkham Notch.*

*A daring jump off 40-foot Garfield Falls near Pittsburg, in the North Country.*

*Beede Falls in Sandwich Notch. This unusual waterfall provides a fine swimming hole.*

*The Basin, a 30-foot wide pothole in Franconia Notch, was created over thousands of years by the scouring action of the Pemigewasset River.*

*Pond Brook Falls. This attractive series of cascades is formed by an eastern tributary of Nash Stream between Groveton and Stark.*

*Cold water and even colder temperatures are at work building an ice shield across Liberty Cascade in Franconia Notch.*

# Winter Activities

When winter snows blanket the mountains and the lakes freeze over, it's time for skiing, snowshoeing, snowmobiling, ice climbing and ice fishing. From Gunstock Ski Area in the Lakes Region, to Waterville Valley, Loon and Cannon in the southern White Mountains, to Wildcat Ski Area in the north, many options await skiers. When the ski areas close in the spring, diehard skiers can tackle the extreme slopes of Tuckerman Ravine. Snowmobilers have excellent trail networks in the Lakes Region and the White Mountain National Forest. Farther north, around Colebrook and Pittsburg—the "North Country"—snowmobiling is the winter activity. Ice fishing and ice boating are popular on Lake Winnipesaukee, and ice climbers find plenty to keep them busy on the cliffs in Franconia Notch and Crawford Notch.

*A snowboarder descends Vista Way at Cannon Mountain. Mount Lafayette and Franconia Ridge rise serenely in the distance.*

*With its thick ice, Alton Bay on Lake Winnipesaukee turns into a bona fide airstrip during the winter months.*

*The annual Pond Hockey Tournament on Meredith Bay brings hundreds of hockey players to the area.*

*This once familiar activity—harvesting lake ice to supply refrigeration for "ice boxes" throughout the summer—is kept alive here on Squam Lake.*

*Sled dog races on Lake Chocorua are a popular winter pastime.*

*The winter view of Squam Lake from West Rattlesnake Mountain.*

Facing page: *In winter, Franconia Notch's Bike Path is an important snowmobile corridor.*

*From high on Mount Washington, two hikers peer into the huge glacially-formed valley known as the Great Gulf.*

Facing page: *A lone hiker contemplates the fantastic
rime ice display on Mount Washington's summit.*

*Located on the grounds of the Mount Washington Hotel, the Bretton Woods Nordic Center boasts 100 kilometers of cross-country ski trails, making it one of the largest in New England.*

*From Lion Head, this spring skier evaluates the various routes in Tuckerman Ravine. His profile lines up with the Center Wall, while the less extreme Left Gully is to the left of him.*

*Protected from mountain winds, Flume Gorge is a perfect place to practice ice climbing.*

*An intrepid skier near the summit of Mount Moosilauke in full winter conditions.*

*Ice boaters fly down Lake Winnipesaukee.*

*The Ice Castle in Lincoln is a man-made winter attraction that allows for any number of photographic opportunities. In this image, one of the employees posed in full ice climbing gear.*

*A skier takes a break from the arduous three-mile trek to Tuckerman Ravine's headwall, still high above him.*